BOSTON RED SOX

MOLLIE MARTIN

CREATIVE EDUCATION

The modern Red Sox continue to hustle just like the legends of old. Here, Jerry Remy chases a Seattle base thief.

Library of Congress Cataloging in Publication Data

Martin, Mollie.
  Boston Red Sox.

  Summary: A history of the Red Sox, from their first game, and first win, on May 8, 1901, through five World Series championships to the present.
  1. Boston Red Sox (Baseball team)—History—Juvenile literature. [1. Boston Red Sox (Baseball team) 2. Baseball—History] I. Title.
GV875.B62M27 1982   796.357'64'0974461   82-13977
ISBN 0-87191-854-4

BOSTON
RED SOX

*A SUIT-ABLE
PRICE*
*Cy Young began
his baseball career
with Canton,
Ohio's team in
the minor Tri-State
league. He made
his jump to the
pros in 1890, when
he was sold to the
National League
team in Cleveland.
In return for the
services of this
future Hall of
Fame pitcher, the
Canton owner
received $300
and a new suit
of clothes!*

Boston, the capital of Massachusetts, is a city with many nicknames and traditions.

It's called "Beantown" in honor of those famous, gooey, juicy, Boston baked beans—a New England favorite.

It's called The Hub of the Universe—or "The Hub", for short—because it has some of America's best schools, libraries and museums.

And it's called "The Cradle of Liberty" because of its big role in the American Revolution. (Paul Revere's midnight ride started here one April night more than 200 years ago.)

But there's another piece of Boston history that is still going strong. Baseball, the All-American pastime, has been an extra-special topic here for the past 80 years.

In 1903, it was, "Did you hear the news? There's a newfangled baseball league in town, and we've got one of the teams!"

In 1914, they said, "Have you seen that big new pitcher the Sox got? Name's Babe Ruth."

In 1941, you'd hear, "I'll bet big Ted Williams will hit .400 this year."

In 1966, it was, "Can you believe it? We finished ninth!" The next year, "Can you believe it? We won the pennant!"

Naturally, today's Bostonians look back with pride on the glorious record of their team. Since 1901, the Red Sox have

A rare photo of Babe Ruth sliding into base. Usually, the Babe took his time prancing easily across home plate.

been one of the most colorful squads in the American League. They've won eight A.L. pennants and five World Series crowns. Boston's rosters have included some of baseball's greatest superstars:

- Fifteen members of the Hall of Fame
- Eight Most Valuable Players
- Fifteen batting champs
- Thirteen home-run champs
- Sixteen runs-batted-in champs
- Thirty-nine pitchers who won 20 games or more

Those records didn't come easy to the team from Boston. In fact, in the year 1900, it looked like there wouldn't be a Red Sox team at all.

THE PILGRIMS HAVE LANDED

The National League of Professional Baseball began in 1876. But the American League—the Red Sox league—didn't get going until 1900.

At first, the American League threatened to rob the National League of its best players by offering higher salaries. It wasn't until 1903 that the two leagues signed a truce.

In the meantime, however, the American League's team in Boston was wasting no time. The team's nickname then was the Pilgrims, in honor of the first settlers who landed on

IN THE BIG INNING . . . Poor Merle Adkins. On July 8, 1902, the pleasant Red Sox pitcher walked to the mound for the start of the sixth inning. It became the longest inning — 16 batters — in Red Sox history.

Ted Williams, the Red Sox legendary home run king, was an electric fielder, too. Here he is in 1939 field action.

9

the shores of Massachusetts at Plymouth Rock almost three centuries earlier. Pilgrim owners built the team's roster in the same way other American League teams built theirs—by offering higher salaries to the players.

First they signed fiery third baseman Jimmy Collins, as player-manager. Then, in a real steal, they lured pitcher Cy Young away from St. Louis. Next, they picked up "Big Bill" Dinneen. another pitching ace. Finally, they landed able infielders Fred Parent and Hobe Ferris, plus outfielders Chick Staht and Buck Freeman. Now the Pilgrims were set for their first big season.

In the very first game Boston fans rallied around their team. A giant crowd was on hand May 8, 1901, when Cy Young's pitching (and 19 Boston hits) beat the Philadelphia Athletics, 12-4. The Pilgrims had landed.

Boston finished second in the American League in 1901, and third in 1902, before coming out on top in 1903. The Pilgrims won 91 out of 138 games that season, and then met the National League's Pittsburgh Pirates in the first game between league champions. It wouldn't officially be called the World Series for two more years, but in the minds of the players, it was the world championship. The Pilgrims won five games . . . the Pirates won three . . . and Boston fans had a winner.

On August 16, 1940, big Jim Foxx broke Lou Gehrig's home run mark, hitting his 31st homer of the season with this mighty swing.

It was more of the same in 1904. The Pilgrims won 95 games and the American League pennant. This time, however, the National League refused to play a championship game. An official World Series agreement was worked out the following year, but Boston would have to wait until 1912 to win the pennant again and take another shot at the world championship.

SOME LEGENDS ARE BORN

Those first Boston teams included some of baseball's all-time great players.

Leading the pitchers, of course, was Denton "Cy" Young. When he first turned pro, the mighty right-handed hurler was a wide-eyed youngster from Tuscarawas County in Ohio. His pants cuffs stopped above his ankles.

On the pitcher's mound, however, Cy was a terror. Batters could only shake their heads in frustration. Young didn't try to strike them out, but he could make them ground out or fly out better than anyone around.

Cy Young was 33-years-old when he joined Boston. Before he retired, he had won 511 career games, including 20 or more wins in 14 straight seasons. In all, Young spent 11 years in the National League and 11 years in the American League. This made him one of the most durable pitchers

The old-timers get together. Shown here are Joe Wood (left), Cy Young, Lefty Grove and Walter Johnson in 1939 reunion at Boston.

HOW CY GOT HIS NICKNAME

"When I began my career, I thought I had to show all my stuff to the coaches and managers," Cy Young remembered. *"I threw the ball so hard I tore a couple of boards off the grandstand. One of the fellows said the stand looked like a cyclone struck it. That's how I got the name that was later shortened to Cy."*

13

ever. In 1956, when a pitching award was established to honor the best in the A.L. and the N.L., it could have but one name: The Cy Young Award. Today, it is still the most valued honor a pitcher can receive.

Young wasn't the only pitching star in Boston. Big Bill Dinneen won 21 games in 1902 and again in 1903; Tom Hughes won 21 in 1903; and Jesse Tannehill notched 22 victories in 1905.

Then, in 1908, "Smokey Joe" Wood joined Boston. The team was now known as the Red Sox because of the bright stockings worn with their uniforms. Wood warmed up in 1911 by winning 23 games. In 1912, he caught fire. That was the year Smokey Joe went 34-5, a season most pitchers would never dream of.

Backing up Wood in 1912 was an outfield some say was the best ever. Tristam E. Speaker led the trio. His teammates called him "Spoke," and later, "The Gray Eagle." Speaker's great speed and anticipation made him perhaps the finest defensive centerfielder in history. He could hit, too. His career batting average was .344, and he stroked a record 793 doubles.

Tris Speaker was a daring outfielder. He invented a special type of centerfield play that no one had ever seen, and few

Boston's Tris Speaker (part of the most famous outfield in Boston history) as he looked in 1912.

14

have tried since. Speaker played very shallow in centerfield, so close to the infield that sometimes he even took pickoff throws at second base from the pitcher! When a long ball was hit, Speaker would judge where it was going, turn and run full speed to where it would drop, and make the catch. Pitchers loved to have Speaker on their teams because he could get outs on short flies and long balls just as well.

Harry Hooper and Duffy Lewis played on either side of Speaker in the outfield. Along with Wood, these men formed the core of the famous 1912 Boston team that won 105 games—a team record that still stands today—for another A.L. pennant.

A large role in that tremendous season was played by a part of the Red Sox club that is still there today. It's called Fenway Park, and in 1912, it replaced Boston's Huntington Avenue Grounds as the Sox' home field.

Fenway is not a huge stadium. Its official seating capacity is just 33,538. But Boston fans have consistently filled Fenway for 70 years to keep the Red Sox among the A.L. attendance leaders.

Fenway's size works to its team's advantage, too. Stands filled with cheering fans loom over opponents who aren't used to such close confines.

They came together in 1939 to play an old-timer's game. Harry Hooper (left), Tris Speaker and Duffy Lewis.

10 OR MORE IN ONE GAME
Six pitchers, all right-handers, struck out 10 or more batters in one game for the Red Sox at least eight times. Smoky Joe Wood did it 18 times, followed by Jim Lonborg and Ray Culp 10 times. Dutch Leonard did it four times — the most for a Red Sox lefty.

THE DAY BABE WALKED OUT ON A PERFECT GAME

Babe Ruth was a great pitcher, but he was also moody. On May 23, 1917, Ruth's first four pitches to Washington's Ray Morgan were called balls by umpire Brick Owens. Ruth stormed off the pitcher's mound, and Owens threw him out of the game. Ernie Shore came on in relief and retired the next 26 men in order for a perfect game!

The 105 wins in 1912 again sent the Sox into the World Series, this time against the New York Giants. And it was just more of the same in the Series, as the team from The Big Apple lost to the team from The Hub, three games to four.

The roster stayed pretty much the same as Boston won two more Series in 1915 and 1916 over Philadelphia.

In 1918 they won yet another Series, whipping a powerful Chicago team, 4-2. Boston hurling ace Carl Mays chipped in an heroic 20 wins that season. But the biggest Boston sensation at that time was a young pitcher named George Herman "Babe" Ruth.

Ruth pitched 16 scoreless innings in the 1916 World Series. In 1918 he ran that string to 29 innings. One day, the Babe asked Boston owner Harry Frazee to switch him to the outfield so he could concentrate on hitting.

"I would be the laughingstock of the league," Frazee said, "if I took the best pitcher in the league and put him in the outfield." Finally, Harry Hooper, a member of that famous Boston outfield, talked Frazee into giving Ruth a chance. That chance changed the face of baseball. In the years to

In a typical 1948 game, Fenway Park was packed to the rafters. Ted Williams hit .369 that year to lead the league.

18

come, Babe Ruth would develop into the greatest home-run hitter of all time, earning for himself the famous nickname, "The Sultan of Swat."

RED SOX FOR SALE

Although the Boston team finished sixth in 1919, the fans had everything to look forward to—or so they thought. Unfortunately, the darkest time for the team was just around the corner.

When Harry Frazee bought the Red Sox in 1916, Boston was in the middle of its most successful stretch—four World Series wins in seven years. Today, Harry Frazee is thought of as a villain in New England because of what he finally did to the Red Sox.

Frazee's first love was the theater. When he purchased the Red Sox, he already owned Frazee Theatre, located in New York City. That was the first bad omen for Boston fans. Worse yet, the theater was located only two doors away from the office of the New York Yankees. As they say in the theater business, it was "curtains" for the Red Sox.

The trouble began in 1919, when Frazee sold Carl Mays, Jake Ruppert and Cap Huston to the Yankees for $40,000 and two unknown pitchers. Frazee soon realized that he could sell players to the Yanks whenever he needed extra

FRAZEE'S LAST LAUGH
Harry Frazee finally did make his mark in the theater. Shortly after he sold the Red Sox, Frazee's theater put on a production of "No, No, Nanette," which became a smash sensation.

In 1973 Duffy Lewis, the famous Red Sox outfielder, was the only man alive who had seen Babe Ruth hit his first and last homers.

money. As it turned out, he needed that cash frequently, to help support his troubled theater.

Over the next few years, Frazee dealt away the entire core of the Red Sox to the Yankees: hard-hitting catcher Wally Schang; future Hall of Fame pitcher Waite Hoyt; shortstop Everett Scott; pitchers "Bullet Joe" Bush, "Sad Sam" Jones, Herb Pennock and George Pipgras; third baseman Joe Dugan, and, finally, even mighty Babe Ruth.

The Yankees now began one of the greatest baseball dynasties in history. But the poor Red Sox sank into a losing streak that would last nearly 20 years. In fact, from 1919 to 1937, Boston never finished higher than fourth in the American League. Nine of those years the once-mighty Red Sox finished dead last.

THE BIG COMEBACK

Things looked pretty hopeless for the Red Sox. But in 1933, Boston hit another turning point. That was the year Thomas Austin Yawkey bought the club.

It didn't happen overnight. Few teams ever go from last to first in one season. But Tom Yawkey began the Boston comeback in 1933 with an "open checkbook" policy. Quite simply, Yawkey made up his mind to buy the best available players. Cost was no object.

In 1932, while making his mark as a Yankee, Babe Ruth recalled his earlier years as a Red Sox pitcher.

AT HOME IN EVERY PARK
In 1919, Babe Ruth hit a record 29 home runs — more than any entire team in baseball!

First Yawkey brought catcher Rick Ferrell and his brother, Wes, a good pitcher, to Boston. The he bartered with Philadelphia and came away with the two future Hall-of-Famers—pitcher Lefty Grove and slugger Jimmie Foxx. It was just the beginning. Just as the Yankees once found a source of great players in Boston, the Red Sox now found a source of its own in Philadelphia. In the 1930s, the A's sent Rube Walberg, Max Bishop, Bing Miller, Dib Williams, Louis Finney, Doc Cramer, Eric McNair and Mike "Pinky" Higgins to The Hub. The rest of the owners were shocked when Yawkey spent $250,000 to bring Joe Cronin to the Red Sox organization. But, as the next 25 years would show, Cronin's playing and managing talents were worth much more.

While Yawkey was busy buying talent, the Red Sox were also busy developing home-grown stars. As it turned out, Boston's cornerstone for years to come was formed by such players, including Bobby Doerr, Johnny Pesky, Boo Ferriss, Tex Hughson, Dom DiMaggio, Mel Parnell and Vern Stephens.

Oh yes, there's one more player who came to the Red Sox in the 1930s. Without him, Boston had already moved from the A.L. cellar to the middle of the pack. With him,

Boston's cornerstone in the 1930's was made up of home-grown talent like Johnny Pesky (left), Vern Stephens, Bobby Doerr and Billy Goodman.

LEFT-HANDED HUMOR

Lefty Grove always had a good sense of humor. Once, when he was playing for the Yankees, he faced slugger Jimmie Foxx, the strongest man in the league. Bill Dickey was catching for New York. Seeing Groves concern, Dickey paced out to the mound. "What do you want to throw this guy?" Dickey asked Grove. 'To tell you the truth, Bill," Lefty replied, "I don't want to throw him anything at all!"

until his retirement in 1960, the Red Sox again became challengers for the pennant—and once, for the World Series. His name? Ted Williams.

TED WILLIAMS TAKES OVER

Spring, 1939. The Red Sox again were gathering in Boston for spring training. The previous season, Cronin, Foxx, Grove and Doerr had led the Sox to a second-place finish in the A.L. This was the team's best showing since its 1918 World Series win. Hopes were high, as word from the scouts came back about a minor-league find named Ted Williams.

He hardly looked the part of a Superstar. Theodore Samuel Williams of San Diego, Calif., stood 6' 3" but weighed only 145 pounds. The Boston uniform hung like an empty bag on his scrawny body. His teammates shook their heads when they saw his rail-thin arms wielding the bat. They almost laughed out loud when they saw him run the bases. It was more like a bouncing gallop, really, or like a girl skipping rope. And, of course, the Red Sox were shocked when, at an early practice, a teammate warned Williams, "Wait'll you see Foxx hit, kid," and Williams replied, "Wait until Foxx sees me hit."

Cocky? Sure. Scared? You Bet. Williams had dreamed of nothing else but batting since he was nine years old. He was

Ted Williams' smooth powerful swing thrilled millions of Red Sox fans during the 1940s and 50s.

a shy loner who disliked drinking, smoking and partying. He had made up for his shyness by building himself up to be a great hitter. This was his big chance in the big leagues. "What if I fail?" he thought. "What will people think of me then?"

When Williams arrived in Boston, a clubhouse assistant said to him, "Oh, well, The Kid has arrived, eh?" The nickname stuck. Before long, The Kid's smooth-stroking, powerful swing was impressing even the veterans.

For the next seven seasons, the Red Sox took a roller-coaster ride along the A.L. team standings. They bounced around between second and seventh, but a pennant never had their name on it. Many of the players (including Williams) took time during this period to fight for their country in World War II. Though the Red Sox fans were frustrated about their team's poor showing, they were much more concerned with the cause of peace.

ANOTHER BOSTON PENNANT

Fortunately, everything fell back into place for the Red Sox in 1946. The war was over. The players were back together, and enthusiasm was riding high. This year the fans would not be disappointed. Another A.L. pennant would be delivered to Fenway Park. Here's how it happened:

Lefty Grove as he appeared in his last year of baseball. The powerful Boston hurler ran up 743 strikeouts in his career.

THE EYES HAVE IT

When Ted Williams was given a physical examination to enter the armed services for World War II, doctors discovered he had 20-10 vision — superior eyesight. But Williams himself believed that his sight was nothing that special. "When I was young, I couldn't see well. The reason I saw the baseball so well was because I was <u>intent</u> on seeing it."

Boston's hitting, which had always been good, was now backed up by strong pitching, led by Dave "Boo" Ferriss. Somehow, the Yankees lost their old hex over the Sox. After New York beat Boston 12-5 early in the season, the Red Sox reversed the score the very next day — and went on to win 15 straight games. By season's end, Boston had won 104 games, just one short of its 1912 record.

In the National League, Los Angeles and St. Louis tied for first and had to play three extra games to break the deadlock. Boston manager Joe Cronin, hoping to keep his team finely tuned, arranged for the Red Sox to play three exhibition games against the A.L. All-Stars. As it turned out, that plan probably cost Boston the 1946 World Series.

In the very first game, Williams was at the plate when veteran pitcher Nickey Haefner threw an inside curve that Williams couldn't avoid. It smashed into his right elbow and sent terrible pain through his entire arm. X-rays showed that the elbow wasn't broken, but it was swollen to three times its normal size.

The injury slowed Ted down during the Series, and St. Louis won it, four games to three. Cardinal pitcher Harry "The Cat" Brecheen won three of those games, handing Boston its first World Series loss ever.

Men of iron. Joe Cronin (left) and Jimmie Foxx were all-time Red Sox sluggers.

THE KID RETIRES

Boston's thrills—and disappointments—were far from over. In 1947, the Red Sox finished third, followed by two heartbreaking second places in 1948 and 1949.

Then the real drought hit. From 1949 to 1967 the scrappy Red Sox never finished above third. It wasn't that they weren't trying. With Williams leading the way, they played their hearts out. But The Kid was again called to serve his country, this time for the Korean War. Though he sparked the Red Sox batting statistics again after he returned, he could never guide them to a World Series win.

In 1960, Williams announced his retirement. He played his last game against Baltimore in Fenway Park, in front of fans and sportswriters who had cheered him on for 22 years. Big No. 9 had walked once and flied out twice when he stepped into the batter's box in the eighth inning.

The first pitch was high. Ball one! The second pitch, a shoulder-high fastball, came whistling over the outside corner of home plate. Williams swung. Strike one!

Then the Baltimore pitcher, 21-year-old Jack Fisher, who was born the same year Williams first reported to spring training, made a memorable mistake: He threw the same pitch again.

Williams holds his silver bat, presented to him for the 1957 batting championship.

Williams pulled the bat around in his classic swing, and—craaack!—the ball took off like a rifle shot. Up and out it sailed. Finally, the Oriole outfielders saw the ball sail over their heads. When it finally returned to earth, it rattled among the deep right-centerfield bleachers. Ted Williams had hit a home run in his last turn at bat!

The crowd in Fenway Park went berserk. All except Ted Williams, that is. Calmly, The Kid rounded the bases and returned to the dugout, just as he had the 520 other times he had hit major-league home runs. No tip of the cap, no wild waving or hand slapping. Williams had stuck to his habits for 22 years, and he wasn't about to break any of them now.

The next day, reality sunk in. "We'll never have anyone like Williams to cheer for again," cried the fans. "Who can we write about now?" asked the sportswriters.

Little did they know that the very next year, another rookie would break into Williams' left-field spot in the Boston lineup—and yet another era in Red Sox history would begin.

THE IMPOSSIBLE DREAM

Everyone called Carl Yastrzemski "Yaz". He wasn't a clone of Ted Williams. He wasn't as tall, and he didn't have The Kid's strength or power. But he did have Williams'

When mighty Ted Williams (right) retired in 1960, rookie Carl Yastrzemski (left) stepped in and took his place.

creamy smooth swing and, more important, a total dedication to the game.

Many times during his long career with the Red Sox, Yaz played with injury and pain. Once, when he had pulled both Achilles tendons, he had the Red Sox trainer tape his feet so he could still play. "They were taped so tight," Yaz recalled, "I had to look down at my feet to make sure they were still there."

Another time, wrist and back injuries prevented him from keeping a grip on his bat. Instead of resting, Yaz considered taping his hands to the bat. He dropped the idea when it occurred to him: "What if I got a hit, and had to run the bases with the bat still taped to my hands?"

Over the years, Yaz would batter the book of batting records. But the first half of the 1960s was not a happy time for him or the Red Sox. From 1961 through 1966, they won 434 games, but lost 625. They finished sixth (in the new 10-team league) once, seventh once, and eighth and ninth two times each. Some called them "The Country Club Sox" because of their reputation for off-the-field antics that affected their play. Overpaid and underworked—that's how much of the league looked at Boston in those days.

After a ninth-place finish in 1966, no one expected much of the '67 team. But, as in 1946, the pieces came together

For over 20 years Yastrzemski whistled homers for the Red Sox. Shown here in 1975 World Series action.

MR. CONSISTENCY Carl Yastrzemski has been steady as a rock. He is, in fact, the only American League player ever to get 100 hits per season his first 20 years.

like a well-cut jigsaw puzzle. The year 1967 was The Year of the Impossible Dream in Boston. The team skyrocketed from next-to-last one season to the World Series the next! Yaz didn't do it alone, of course. Dick Williams, the new Red Sox manager, erased the team's "country club" image with a strict set of rules that let the players concentrate on baseball. Jim Lonborg, a Cy Young Award-winning pitcher was on the mound. In the outfield it was Reggie Smith and Tony Conigliaro who sparked the team. In the infield it was shortstop Rico Petrocelli and burly first baseman George Scott who set the pace.

As with most Boston teams, pitching wasn't the real Red Sox strength in 1967. But there seemed to be something magical about their hitting. Day after day, game after game, the Red Sox were able to put as many runs up on the scoreboard as the Boston pitcher needed for the win. It might be one run one day and 12 the next.

The A.L. pennant didn't come easy to the Red Sox. They began the season red-hot, slumped before the break for the All-Star game, then put together a 10-game winning streak.

Then, on August 18, tragedy struck. Conigliaro couldn't duck away from an inside fastball. It struck him squarely below his left eye, fracturing his cheekbone. At the time,

Boston hustle. Rightfielder Reggie Smith piles into the padded wall in pursuit of this pesky 1972 double.

Tony C. was leading the league in home runs. The injury knocked him out of the '67 season, and Conigliaro never really played the same caliber of ball again.

Tony's injury damaged team morale. Even Yaz, who had a Superman year, went 0-for-18 at the plate in one stretch. Still, with one week remaining in the regular '67 season, Boston was still tied for first with Minnesota. Chicago and Detroit were close behind. When Boston lost two straight, the fans smelled doom. But, somehow the Red Sox pulled together to win their final three. The Impossible Dream had come true.

After such a closely-fought pennant race, the 1967 World Series was almost a letdown for Boston. The St. Louis Cardinals, the N.L. champion, was everybody's pick to win the title, which they did, but the Red Sox took the Red Birds to seven games.

St. Louis fireballer Bob Gibson met Lonborg in the deciding contest in Fenway Park. When the Red Sox came to bat in the bottom of the ninth, they trailed, 7-2, and it was a sure bet that St. Louis would be world champ. Still, each seat in Fenway was bare as every Boston fan was on his feet, cheering the Red Sox not only for that day's performance, but for the entire season.

Tony takes his cuts. Popular Tony Conigliaro was injured by a pitch in 1967. Here at the 1975 training camp, he tries his comeback.

LOVE THOSE 1970'S
The decade of the 70's was a great one for the Red Sox. They won the pennant in 1975 and just missed in 1972, '77, and '78.

As Tom Yawkey would say later, "No, I can't say the World Series of '67 was a great disappointment. Not after the great year they gave us."

THE CHANGING GUARD

The Impossible Dream couldn't last forever. The very next season, the Red Sox dropped to fourth place, followed by three thirds in following years. In 1972 and again in 1973, the club scored two second-place finishes. That familiar "middle-of-the-pack" position was back again.

Boston fans still had plenty to cheer about, though. In 1972, rookie catcher Carlton Fisk won Rookie of the Year honors.

Ageless Luis Tiant baffled batters with pitches that would help him earn the Comeback Player of the Year Award.

Tommy Harper cemented his reputation as one of base-ball's trickiest base-stealers.

In 1975, rookie Jim Rice batted .309, hit 22 home runs and 102 RBIs. As great as Rice was, he was overshadowed by his own Boston teammate, Fred Lynn, another rookie who batted .331 and was named Rookie of the Year and Most Valuable Player.

In receiving his awards, Lynn tipped his cap to Rice's hitting. And rightfully so!

Red Sox catcher Carlton Fisk, the 1972 Rookie of the Year, stops to pose for a shot at the '79 training camp.

Jim Rice seems to be made in the mold of former Red Sox slugger Jimmie Foxx. Rice brings awesome power to the plate with his short, flat swing. Stand alongside the batting cage and you can actually hear his bat whistle through the air. Once, he snapped a bat in half just by checking his swing.

'My strength," says Rice, "comes from my wrists and legs. But then I bring my left shoulder back so that all my momentum jumps out to the ball. It's like a rattlesnake—he coils and springs out."

In 1975, with Rice, Yaz, Harper, Fisk and Lynn playing tightly, Boston jumped to first in the new Eastern Division of the American League. They then blanked the three-time defending World Series champions, the Oakland A's, three games to zero, for the A.L. pennant. Next: the World Series and the Cincinnati Reds.

Boston entered the Series without Rice, who had broken his wrist late in the season. Pete Rose led the Reds with a .370 Series batting average, but the seven-game series was a classic matchup of teams, not individuals.

Five of the seven games were decided by one run. In the last battle, the Reds scored in the top of the ninth inning for the final winning margin, 4-3.

A big sigh whistled through New England that fall. Eight

His bat strikes like a snake. Awesome home-run hitter Jim Rice powers one out against the Yanks in '79.

HITTING FOR THE CYCLE
One of baseball's most unusual feats occurs when a batter hits for the "cycle" — scoring a single, double, triple and a home run in the same game. Over the years, thirteen Red Sox players have hit for the cycle. The latest was Fred Lynn on May 13, 1980.

YAZ AND HIS
BIG RBI
In 1981, Carl
Yastrzemski —
the aging
superstar — hit
more game-
winning RBI
than any other
player on the
Red Sox team. In
all, Yaz
polished off ten
games for the
Birds in this
manner.

times since 1901, the Boston Red Sox had played for the title of World Series champion. The first five times, the Red Sox won; the last three Series each ended in 4-3 losses.

THE FUTURE LOOKS GOOD

Today's Red Sox fans have three "generations" of Boston players leading the team. First and foremost is Carl Yastrzemski, who completed his 21st pro season in 1981. Yaz is the single remaining "Impossible Dreamer", a mature player with the skill and character to help others realize what is truly possible.

There are other Boston veterans, among them powerful outfielder Jim Rice and slick second baseman Jerry Remy.

Finally, there are the newcomers. Some, like Frank Tanana, Joe Rudi and Tony Perez are veterans. Others, like exciting pitcher Bob Ojeda, are rookies.

With talent like this, and with the commitment of the Red Sox management—President Jean Yawkey, Executive Vice Presidents Haywood Sullivan and Edward Leroux—Boston fans have good reason to expect great things in years to come. A World Series championship every season would be nice. But, win or lose, Boston fans know they can count on their team for a total effort. Boston teams have always had Boston pride. It's old, deep and sturdy. Like Boston itself.

Luis Tiant was called "the man of many motions" by frustrated batters who faced the Red Sox righthander in the '70s.

Frank Tanana pitched with an inflamed left arm, but he won this 1981 contest against Oakland.